Bird Mandalas & Painted Moments

ADULT COLORING BOOK WITH POETRY AND SELF-DISCOVERY

Aventuras De Viaje

Copyright SF Nonfiction Books © 2024

All Rights Reserved

No part of this document may be reproduced without written consent from the author.

www.SFNonfictionBooks.com

INTRODUCTION

Welcome to an enchanting aviary, where the splendor of exotic birds merges with the vibrant dance of colors. This coloring book is more than a collection of images; it's a journey into the heart of nature's most flamboyant creatures.

In these pages, the exotic allure of birds from around the globe takes flight. Each bird, with its unique plumage and captivating presence, offers a glimpse into the wondrous diversity of our planet. From the iridescent feathers of a hummingbird to the majestic wingspan of an eagle, these pages celebrate the beauty and mystery of the avian world.

Coloring these intricate designs is an invitation to mindfulness and tranquility. As you fill each page with hues of your choosing, you engage in an act of creative meditation. This process not only stimulates your imagination but also provides a peaceful retreat from the hustle and bustle of daily life. By connecting with the serene essence of these birds, you embark on a personal journey of relaxation and introspection.

Discovering the Mosaic of Imagination

Venture deeper, and you'll discover how this book is intricately designed to enrich your coloring experience:

- **Simple Activities**: Beyond just coloring, engage with activities designed to spark reflection and creativity. These gentle prompts will lead you to moments of introspection, serving as kindling for your inner fire.

- **Quotes**: Let the wisdom of personal development accompany you, illuminating your path as you add your own burst of color to the pages.

- **Positive Affirmations**: As you color, let these words of positivity uplift your spirit, molding your thoughts and inspiring a brighter perspective.

- **Poems and Haikus**: Delight in the poetic tales that complement the theme of this book, capturing life's varied rhythms and experiences. Each verse and every line serve as a muse for your artistic endeavors, enhancing your coloring journey with lyrical inspiration.

Embark on this coloring odyssey, immersing yourself in a world of diverse themes and the therapeutic embrace of art. Each page invites you on a unique journey, blending your creativity with the tranquility of coloring.

THANKS FOR YOUR PURCHASE

Get Your Next SF Nonfiction Book FREE!

Claim the book of your choice at:

www.SFNonfictionBooks.com/Free-Book

You will also be among the first to know of all the latest releases, discount offers, bonus content, and more.

Go to:

www.SFNonfictionBooks.com/Free-Book

Thanks again for your support.

Reflection Space:
Reflect on a moment when you felt as free as a bird.

_____

_____

"With wings of resilience, soar above the storms of life."

In skies uncharted,
Exotic whispers take flight,
Unfurling colors bright.
Each wingbeat, a rhythm,
In the dance of endless skies,
A journey of eyes.

I spread my wings
of hope and soar above the clouds
of doubt.

Birdwatching Prompt:
Spend some time birdwatching and jot down your observations and how it made you feel.

_____

_____

"Let your dreams
take flight, like a bird exploring
the boundless sky."

I cherish the unique melody of my life, as each bird cherishes its own song.

Wings spread, colors bright,
Skyward dreams take swift flight,
Dawn breaks, hearts alight.

Flight Goals:
Write down your "flight goals" for the week, month, or year.

_____

_____

"In every feather, a new story; in every flap, a new journey."

I am open to new horizons,
ready to explore like a bird soaring
high.

Feathered hues of dawn,
Whispering tales of freedom,
In each plume, life's song.

Bird's Eye View:
Sketch or describe a bird's eye view of your life and your goals.

_____

_____

"Exotic birds remind us
to embrace our own unique colors
in a world full of
different feathers."

I am as free and boundless as a bird in flight.

Morning's soft first light,
Colors burst in sky's great height,
Freedom's call takes flight.

Feather Collection:
Start a feather collection, and list the types of feathers you've found.

_____

_____

"Your wings already exist, all you have to do is fly."

I embrace the vibrant colors of my being, just like the exotic birds in the sky.

Soft flutter, dawn's light,
New day beckons, hearts alight,
Dreams take flight, hearts bright.

Wing Span Measurement:
Measure the "wing span" of your ambitions.

_____

_____

"Be like a bird, fearless in the pursuit of what sets your soul free."

I believe in the freedom of expressing my true colors.

Exotic feathers,
In a world of vibrant dreams,
Sky's unending streams.
With every beat, rise higher,
In colors, let hearts aspire,
Life's palette, endless choir.

Freedom List:
List what freedom means to you.

_____

_____

"Embrace the freedom of your unique flight path."

I am on a journey of self-discovery, flying towards my dreams.

Feathers dance on breeze,
Colors sing among the trees,
Life's hues, hearts appease.

Feathered Friends:
Jot down names of supportive friends who help you "soar".

_____

_____

"Feathers may ruffle, wings may tire, but the heart's flight is endless."

I celebrate the dance of life, akin to the fluttering dance of exotic wings.

Birds of paradise,
Nature's vibrant canopy,
Life's boundless surmise.
Sing a tune of hope,
In each hue, find scope,
On sky's broad, endless slope.

Birdsong Reflection:
Listen to birdsong and reflect on its melody and how it resonates with your current life situation.

_____

_____

"With each day, spread your wings of courage and take flight."

I am fearless in my flight towards success.

Bold colors take flight,
In the vast sky, hearts alight,
Dreams soar, pure delight.

**Wings of Change:
Note changes you wish to make in
your life to feel more free.**

_____

_____

"Exotic birds aren't just free; they exemplify freedom."

I flutter towards my dreams with a heart full of hope.

In the heart of woods,
Silence hums a melody,
Birds bring life to trees.
Each flutter, a story,
Of winds that sing of glory,
Nature's territory.

Colorful Experiences:
Color the birds based on your emotions and reflect on the color choices.

_____

_____

"Dance to the rhythm of life, like the exotic birds dance in the sky."

I am a creator of my own destiny, soaring through the sky of possibilities.

Silence breaks with song,
Winged hopes to skies belong,
Life's tune, loud and strong.

Migration Plans:
Detail a plan to "migrate" towards achieving a personal or professional goal.

_____

_____

"Let your hopes, not your hurts, shape your future just as wings shape a bird's journey."

I find joy in the small chirps of happiness life offers.

Beyond the dense veil,
Lie wings unclipped, dreams unchained,
Awaits sky's soft hail.
Among trees, find your guise,
In the open, spirits rise,
Embrace the sunlit skies.

Daily Flights: Note new experiences or learnings of the day, akin to a bird's daily flights.

_____

_____

"Even a caged bird can dream of the sky. Never let circumstances clip your wings."

BEYOND THESE PAGES

A Deeper Dive into Art and Soul Awaits!

This book is but a chapter in a voyage where creativity meets depth.

Craving more? Explore the link below and weave deeper into the tapestry of art and emotion.

www.SFNonfictionBooks.com/Adult-Coloring-Books

A HEARTFELT THANK YOU

As the colors on these pages have come to life, so has our shared journey in this artistic realm. I am deeply grateful for your trust in choosing this book, and more so for allowing it to be a part of your self-care and personal journey.

Taking time for oneself is a gift—a silent promise of growth, introspection, and rejuvenation. By picking up the colors and filling these pages, you've not just created art but have also woven moments of peace, reflection, and creativity into your life.

Thank you for making space for yourself, for embracing the wonders within these pages, and for dancing to the rhythm of the lines and hues within this book. Your journey here is a testament to the beauty of dedicating time to one's soul and spirit.

If you enjoyed this journey and wish to explore more, know that there are other themes awaiting your artistic touch. Dive into new worlds and let your imagination flow.

From the deepest corner of my heart, thank you for bringing this book to life. Until our next artistic adventure together, cherish the colors of your journey and continue to shine.

Warmly,

Aventuras De Viaje

ABOUT THE AUTHOR

Aventuras has three passions: travel, writing, and learning new skills.

Combining these three things, Miss Viaje spends her time exploring the world and learning about anything and everything that interests her, from yoga, to music, to science, and more.

Aventuras takes what she discovers and shares it through her books.

www.SFNonfictionBooks.com

www.ingramcontent.com/pod-product-compliance
Lightning Source LLC
Chambersburg PA
CBHW081725100526
44591CB00016B/2509